ISBN 978-0-331-41732-6
PIBN 11120961

foreign
agriculture
circular

poultry and eggs

BROILERS AND EGGS LED INCREASE IN
U.S. POULTRY EXPORTS IN 1981

FPE 1-82
Marcn 1982

Exports of U.S. poultry products showed substantial increases again in 1981, with a total value that was 27 percent above 1980 sales. Poultry meat accounted for two-thirds of the overall export value in 1981, while eggs and egg products made up about one-fourth of the total, and live poultry exports brought in the remaining value. Chicken parts, whole broilers, table eggs, and egg products accounted for almost all of the increase in the U.S. total export value for poultry in 1981.

Broilers

U.S. exports of chicken parts increased 35 percent over the 1980 level, with the Far East and the Caribbean together taking 73 percent of U.S. exports of chicken parts in 1981. Japan showed the largest 1981 increase as consumer demand continued to climb and Japanese broiler production declined slightly. The average per-ton export value of chicken parts was about 5 percent above the 1980 figure. U.S. exports of whole broilers were 17 percent above the 1980 figure, because large increases to Egypt, Iraq, and Venezuela more than offset the numerous declines in other markets. These three countries and Mexico accounted for 82 percent of U.S. whole broiler exports in 1981. Egypt showed the largest increase last year, as the Egyptian Government continued its high level of meat imports. The average export value of whole broilers increased by less than 2 percent in 1981.

Trade figures point up the difference between the markets for the two categories of U.S. broiler exports, chicken parts and whole broilers, during the last two years. Of the 16 countries that imported at least 1,000 tons of U.S. chicken parts in 1980, two-thirds increased those imports during 1981 and only one country decreased its imports by more than 12 percent. On the other hand, of the 17 countries that imported at least 1,000 tons of U.S. whole broilers in 1980, more than half decreased their imports of this U.S. product during 1981 and seven of these countries showed declines of more than 65 percent. The difference in the markets of these two export categories resulted in large part from the U.S. position relative to other major exporters. The United States is presently, without significant competition, the leading exporter of chicken parts. On the other hand, competition for whole broiler exports, primarily from the EC and Brazil, is intense. For

For further information, contact the U.S. Department of Agriculture, Foreign Agricultural Service, Dairy, Livestock and Poultry Division, Room 6616-South Building, Washington, DC 20250. Telephone (202) 447-8031.

example, U.S. exports of whole broilers to Saudi Arabia, Romania, and Angola dropped drastically in 1981, while French shipments of whole chickens to each of these countries increased substantially last year.

Turkey Parts

U.S. exports of turkey parts in 1981 were 24 percent below the 1980 level, primarily due to declines in the two major U.S. markets, Egypt and West Germany. U.S. shipments to Egypt slowed considerably during the latter half of 1981, probably due to Egyptian restrictions on private sector imports and general confusion regarding Egyptian import policies. U.S. exports to West Germany in 1981 were hurt by the strengthening of the dollar.

Table Eggs

U.S. exports of table eggs increased by 75 percent last year, compared with the 1980 level, and 70 percent of the 1981 total went to the Middle East. The impressive increase in U.S. exports to the Middle East was due to increased demand from oil-producing countries, low U.S. egg prices, and the unique ability of the U.S. industry to fill large export orders quickly. Exports of U.S. table eggs to Hong Kong also rose significantly, probably due to lower shipments from Hong Kong's other major supplier, China. The average export value for U.S. table eggs in 1981 was about 5 percent above the 1980 figure.

Egg Products

U.S. exports of egg products in 1981 were substantially above the 1980 level, primarily as a result of increased exports to Japan. Egg production in Japan declined slightly in 1981, while Japanese confectioners, bakers, and producers of meat and fish pastes increased their demand for egg products.

2

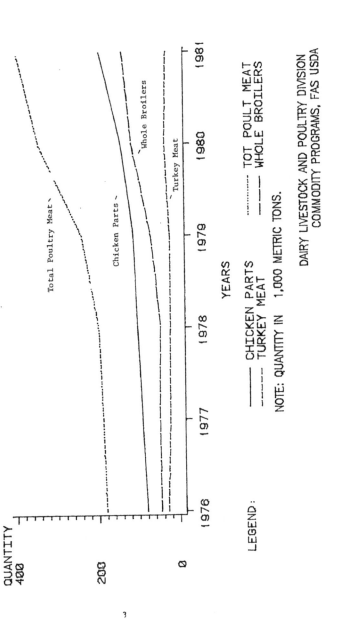

UNITED STATES EXPORTS OF
POULTRY MEAT
1976 — 1981

QUANTITY
400

200

0

    1976   1977   1978   1979   1980   1981

YEARS

Total Poultry Meat

Chicken Parts

Whole Broilers

Turkey Meat

LEGEND:
———— CHICKEN PARTS   ·········· TOT POULT MEAT
– – – – TURKEY MEAT   —— WHOLE BROILERS

NOTE: QUANTITY IN 1,000 METRIC TONS.

DAIRY LIVESTOCK AND POULTRY DIVISION
COMMODITY PROGRAMS, FAS USDA

3

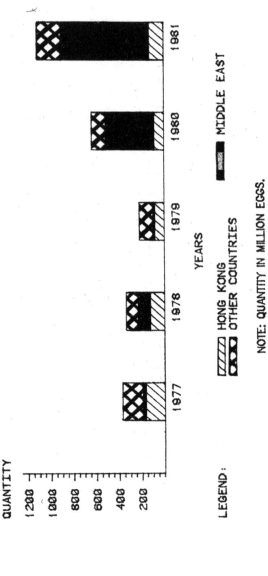

UNITED STATES
EXPORTS OF TABLE EGGS
1977 – 1981

QUANTITY

1200
1000
800
600
400
200

1977   1978   1979   1980   1981

YEARS

LEGEND:

HONG KONG
OTHER COUNTRIES
MIDDLE EAST

NOTE: QUANTITY IN MILLION EGGS.

DAIRY LIVESTOCK AND POULTRY DIVISION

4

TABLE 1.—POULTRY PRODUCTS: U.S. EXPORTS, QUANTITY AND VALUE,
AVERAGE 1974-78, ANNUAL 1979-81

COMMODITY	QUANTITY (IN METRIC TONS UNLESS OTHERWISE SHOWN)				VALUE (IN THOUSANDS OF DOLLARS)			
	5-YEAR AVG 1974-1978	1979	1980	1981 1/	5-YEAR AVG 1974-1978	1979	1980	1981 1/
EXPORTS								
POULTRY MEAT:FRESH, OR FROZEN								
YOUNG CHICKENS 2/	107,494	182,348	257,214	326,203	98,693	195,492	293,471	382,064
FOWL	7,181	14,476	23,196	17,842	8,554	16,876	25,833	22,752
TURKEYS	23,310	22,685	34,049	28,569	31,694	37,123	46,177	44,924
POULTRY MEAT, NEC	5,293	9,815	14,977	5,973	5,886	11,961	21,051	16,506
POULTRY LIVERS	2,410	3,556	2,549	3,164	2,610	3,164	24,689	3,598
POULTRY SPECIALTIES 3/	1,669	3,427	5,152	7,249	2,358	6,971	11,425	11,435
TOTAL	147,357	236,307	339,139	393,100	149,364	271,786	409,447	453,677
CANNED POULTRY	2,103	1,756	2,705	1,452	3,277	4,141	4,380	1,398
TOTAL POULTRY MEAT	149,063	238,063	341,843	394,552	151,669	275,927	405,027	407,276
EGGS								
TABLE (IN 1000 DOZEN)	17,995	16,027	52,940	92,807	10,866	11,941	34,680	64,964
HATCHING (IN 1000 DOZEN)	15,366	24,001	26,145	27,247	22,094	39,095	42,608	45,872
DRIED, NEC	1,726	3,134	4,813	7,302	6,857	14,763	28,478	26,478
FROZEN OR OTHERWISE PRES.	4,645	5,516	10,411	27,292	5,874	7,498	18,189	38,885
TOTAL	0	0	0	0	45,691	73,297	124,553	175,219
LIVE POULTRY								
BABY CHICKS (IN THOUSANDS)	26,948	28,056	33,714	39,813	23,292	36,974	43,968	53,556
TURKEY POULTS (IN THOUSANDS)	8,879	1,568	635	1,545	668	1,320	749	1,437
OTHER 4/	5,415	0	0	0	5,496	3,720	3,773	4,280
TOTAL	0	0	0	0	23,366	42,014	48,490	59,252
TOTAL POULTRY AND EGGS 5/	0	0	0	0	227,407	391,638	569,020	722,247

NOTE: TOTALS MAY NOT ADD DUE TO ROUNDING.

1/ PRELIMINARY. 2/ WHOLE OR PARTS. 3/ BEGINNING 1978 INCLUDES BIRDS EXCEPT CANNED. 4/ REPORTED IN POUNDS PRIOR TO 1978. 5/ DOES NOT INCLUDE MEAT FROM SMALL GAME, FEATHERS, AND DOWN.

SOURCE: U.S. DEPARTMENT OF COMMERCE

MARCH 1982

FOREIGN COMMODITY ANALYSIS, FAS, USDA

TABLE 2.--YOUNG CHICKENS, WHOLE FRESH, OR FROZEN: U.S. EXPORTS BY COUNTRY OF DESTINATION

AVERAGE 1974-78, ANNUAL 1979-81

COMMODITY AND COUNTRY OF DESTINATION	QUANTITY (IN METRIC TONS)				VALUE (IN THOUSANDS OF DOLLARS)			
	5-YEAR AVG 1974-1978	1979	1980	1981 1/	5-YEAR AVG 1974-1978	1979	1980	1981 1/
YOUNG CHICKENS,WHOLE,FR/FZN								
NORTH AMERICA:								
BAHAMAS......................	80	164	128	221	117	226	161	277
BARBADOS.....................	58	153	222	54	44	169	249	32
BELIZE.......................	14	11	9	66	14	18	10	99
BERMUDA......................	165	287	106	89	276	496	155	149
CANADA.......................	3,476	3,370	2,562	834	3,939	3,817	2,903	1,065
DOMINICAN REPUBLIC...........	0	1,591	3,747	886	1	1,804	4,543	1,195
HAITI........................	19	1	28	3	31	2	30	5
HONDURAS.....................	2	4	24	22	2	5	29	41
JAMAICA......................	294	5,253	2,612	2,901	367	2,011	1,545	1,296
LEEWARD-WINDWARD IS..........	126	511	426	1,071	134	519	447	758
MEXICO.......................	3,590	6,174	7,175	8,832	3,194	6,245	7,736	10,831
NETHERLANDS ANTILLES.........	451	941	911	342	505	1,003	1,065	505
NICARAGUA....................	5	0	3,438	3,006	5	0	4,047	4,232
PANAMA(INC CANAL ZN).........	16	10	34	14	19	13	29	35
TRINIDAD-TOBAGO..............	45	647	587	351	59	840	914	545
OTHER........................	106	292	163	320	114	372	214	247
TOTAL..................	8,445	19,499	22,170	19,012	8,819	17,621	24,079	21,312
SOUTH AMERICA:								
BRAZIL.......................	30	0	0	0	29	0	0	0
CHILE........................	407	192	171	75	396	212	202	91
COLOMBIA.....................	25	114	346	538	27	123	384	594
SURINAME.....................	0	18	0	0	0	6	0	0
VENEZUELA....................	5,617	21,983	10,940	17,363	5,935	23,129	12,785	25,367
OTHER........................	4	2,632	619	297	4	3,138	713	242
TOTAL..................	6,083	24,940	12,076	18,294	6,390	26,608	14,004	26,295
EUROPE:								
FRANCE.......................	4	0	0	18	5	0	0	29
GERMANY, FEDERAL REP. OF..	38	28	53	18	47	53	53	30
ITALY........................	3	6	26	0	4	18	40	0
NETHERLANDS..................	32	0	22	59	31	0	29	94
UNITED KINGDOM...............	60	403	32	41	125	1,133	68	75
TOTAL EC-9.............	136	438	132	137	212	1,204	189	228
AUSTRIA......................	17	0	0	0	20	0	0	0
GREECE.......................	50	18	43	22	54	22	60	31
ROMANIA......................	0	0	4,725	0	0	0	11,165	0
SWITZERLAND..................	47	132	281	88	56	225	507	140
OTHER........................	1,706	0	31	0	1,821	0	31	0
TOTAL..................	1,956	588	5,212	248	2,162	1,450	11,952	400
AFRICA:								
CANARY ISLANDS...............	36	158	391	295	36	224	353	342
EGYPT........................	1,611	9,745	25,110	52,272	1,680	11,122	28,937	62,787
GUINEA.......................	10	11	10	11	17	25	17	20
LIBERIA......................	10	8	13	88	14	15	19	137
NIGERIA......................	681	2,835	924	1,758	628	3,161	1,026	2,078
OTHER........................	9	82	4,561	929	12	104	5,241	1,436
TOTAL..................	2,357	12,839	30,919	55,354	2,388	14,651	35,594	66,799
ASIA AND OCEANIA:								
BAHRAIN......................	49	75	139	215	91	104	318	456
FRENCH PACIFIC ISLAND.....	718	2,195	2,214	1,296	843	2,804	2,764	1,629
HONG KONG....................	569	412	1,301	906	546	525	1,554	1,124
IRAQ.........................	8,491	0	25,459	31,933	8,658	0	31,797	42,179
JAPAN........................	1,343	1,704	1,653	2,119	1,627	2,163	2,117	2,514
JORDAN.......................	0	0	2,553	8	0	0	2,853	10
KUWAIT.......................	118	126	506	96	168	179	606	130
LEBANON......................	277	10	43	43	284	9	102	54
MALAYSIA.....................	96	0	25	0	77	0	32	0
NEW ZEALAND..................	6	0	5	9	9	0	7	10
QATAR........................	10	7	17	7	14	10	29	13
SAUDI ARABIA.................	221	2,663	7,309	509	370	3,939	10,855	939
SINGAPORE....................	1,067	3,127	2,559	3,366	1,077	3,546	2,905	4,016
TRUST TERRITORY PACIFIC IS	423	614	911	831	461	660	1,103	1,066
UNITED ARAB EMIRATES.........	126	152	77	226	159	303	138	470
WESTERN SAMOA................	116	266	149	63	107	209	165	76
OTHER........................	148	1,245	17	28	193	2,025	27	47
TOTAL..................	13,729	12,596	44,930	41,614	14,684	16,477	57,372	54,734
GRAND TOTAL.............	32,570	78,372	115,316	134,521	34,443	76,807	143,802	169,540

NOTE: TOTALS MAY NOT ADD DUE TO ROUNDING.

1/ PRELIMINARY.

SOURCE: U.S. DEPARTMENT OF COMMERCE

MARCH 1982

FOREIGN COMMODITY ANALYSIS, FAS, USDA

TABLE 3.--FOWL, WHOLE, FRESH, OR FROZEN: U.S. EXPORTS BY COUNTRY OF DESTINATION

AVERAGE 1974-78, ANNUAL 1979-81

COMMODITY AND COUNTRY OF DESTINATION	QUANTITY (IN METRIC TONS)				VALUE (IN THOUSANDS OF DOLLARS)			
	5-YEAR AVG 1974-1978	1979	1980	1981 [1/]	5-YEAR AVG 1974-1978	1979	1980	1981 [1/]
FOWL,WHOLE,FRESH OR FROZEN								
NORTH AMERICA:								
BAHAMAS....................	4	11	13	37	6	22	21	52
BARBADOS..................	0	66	4	169	1	51	11	246
BELIZE....................	1	0	5	9	1	0	6	0
BERMUDA...................	80	8	52	21	145	15	76	45
CANADA....................	3,215	2,112	3,918	4,391	3,460	2,239	4,667	5,499
DOMINICAN REPUBLIC........	0	33	252	0	0	42	336	0
JAMAICA...................	37	0	13	102	33	0	7	172
LEEWARD-WINDWARD IS.......	55	46	108	200	57	69	129	188
MEXICO....................	210	644	305	846	195	679	420	872
NETHERLANDS ANTILLES......	89	89	98	142	95	106	117	191
OTHER.....................	120	2,493	1,006	546	171	3,068	1,540	925
TOTAL................	3,811	5,503	5,854	6,656	4,165	6,291	7,350	8,189
SOUTH AMERICA:								
ARGENTINA.................	0	405	298	0	0	482	467	0
VENEZUELA.................	387	818	1,670	2,904	445	956	2,680	4,128
OTHER.....................	34	268	389	301	41	339	489	447
TOTAL................	422	1,490	2,357	3,205	485	1,778	3,636	4,575
EUROPE:								
BELGIUM-LUXEMBOURG........	0	0	0	3	0	0	0	5
DENMARK...................	0	0	0	0	0	24	0	0
FRANCE....................	0	23	0	0	0	24	0	0
GERMANY, FEDERAL REP. OF..	27	63	41	117	52	92	57	158
ITALY.....................	0	0	0	16	0	0	0	28
NETHERLANDS...............	7	0	8	34	0	0	15	72
UNITED KINGDOM............	0	2	33	99	0	4	19	169
TOTAL EC-9...........	35	89	82	268	62	120	91	431
GREECE....................	3	0	0	12	4	0	0	9
MALTA-GOZO................	6	0	0	0	10	0	0	0
SWITZERLAND...............	21	55	86	120	24	59	71	113
OTHER.....................	18	93	2	394	21	125	2	336
TOTAL................	82	237	151	795	121	304	163	888
AFRICA:								
CANARY ISLANDS............	27	120	319	123	29	139	393	136
EGYPT.....................	0	962	624	430	0	995	937	618
LIBERIA...................	0	0	33	13	0	0	81	17
NIGERIA...................	486	0	3,840	3,002	436	0	4,124	3,516
REP SOUTH AFRICA..........	0	0	291	142	0	0	465	171
OTHER.....................	4	0	0	46	5	0	0	66
TOTAL................	518	1,082	5,308	3,756	470	1,133	5,999	4,524
ASIA AND OCEANIA:								
FRENCH PACIFIC ISLANDS....	286	248	493	999	360	279	665	1,286
HONG KONG.................	100	1,361	367	71	94	1,471	435	87
JAPAN.....................	1,423	3,174	282	620	2,242	3,587	377	873
KUWAIT....................	5	97	56	27	8	132	89	74
NEW ZEALAND...............	2	0	0	0	2	0	0	0
SAUDI ARABIA..............	126	135	7,843	1,280	139	249	6,564	1,398
SINGAPORE.................	238	471	201	165	260	580	210	198
TRUST TERRITORY PACIFIC IS	114	89	202	351	119	96	253	432
WESTERN SAMOA.............	7	7	47	16	6	8	58	17
OTHER.....................	47	582	36	103	62	968	65	209
TOTAL................	2,347	6,164	9,527	3,631	3,293	7,369	8,715	4,575
GRAND TOTAL..............	7,181	14,476	23,196	17,842	8,534	16,876	25,833	22,752

NOTE: TOTALS MAY NOT ADD DUE TO ROUNDING.

1/ PRELIMINARY.

SOURCE: U.S. DEPARTMENT OF COMMERCE

MARCH 1982

FOREIGN COMMODITY ANALYSIS, FAS, USDA

COMMODITY AND COUNTRY OF DESTINATION	QUANTITY (IN METRIC TONS)				VALUE (IN THOUSANDS OF DOLLARS)			
	5-YEAR AVG 1974-1978	1979	1980	1981 1/	5-YEAR AVG 1974-1978	1979	1980	1981 1/
CHICKEN PARTS,FRESH/FROZEN								
NORTH AMERICA:								
BAHAMAS...................	41	132	175	198	73	205	273	272
BARBADOS..................	1,792	2,549	2,622	2,388	847	2,126	2,697	2,519
BELIZE....................	8	10	16	32	4	14	28	51
BERMUDA...................	837	994	1,183	1,248	1,310	1,606	1,932	2,136
CANADA....................	2,300	4,521	4,182	4,623	2,093	4,717	5,580	7,269
DOMINICAN REPUBLIC........	81	53	80	23	53	46	77	20
FRENCH WEST INDIES........	34	75	53	33	38	99	64	43
HONDURAS..................	7	0	11	0	4	0	17	0
JAMAICA...................	12,747	10,569	13,734	19,106	4,591	4,104	4,053	5,799
LEEWARD-WINDWARD IS.......	4,889	9,249	8,769	10,545	2,941	7,511	7,513	9,410
MEXICO....................	1,189	3,762	5,428	10,902	622	2,864	4,829	13,203
NETHERLANDS ANTILLES......	3,187	4,512	3,927	5,084	3,431	5,574	4,969	6,398
PANAMA(INC CANAL ZN)......	11	11	0	69	13	17	0	95
TRINIDAD-TOBAGO...........	115	568	402	752	106	611	487	931
OTHER.....................	71	160	418	356	96	214	435	476
TOTAL..................	27,308	37,164	41,020	55,271	16,223	29,797	32,951	48,623
SOUTH AMERICA:								
BRAZIL....................	3	0	0	0	2	0	1	0
CHILE.....................	15	69	459	2,589	9	91	534	2,315
COLOMBIA..................	10	9	26	111	3	14	26	106
PERU......................	0	0	46	0	0	0	29	0
SURINAME..................	128	30	0	0	54	20	0	0
OTHER.....................	40	277	1,197	4,259	41	320	1,459	5,980
TOTAL..................	196	385	1,731	6,959	109	445	2,051	8,401
EUROPE:								
BELGIUM-LUXEMBOURG........	116	14	156	120	149	19	182	118
DENMARK...................	10	0	0	0	17	0	0	0
FRANCE....................	46	0	43	174	34	0	40	210
GERMANY, FEDERAL REP. OF..	335	100	485	322	485	141	653	377
IRELAND...................	0	16	0	0	0	24	0	0
ITALY.....................	182	119	140	0	215	207	174	0
NETHERLANDS...............	237	446	667	1,399	233	542	981	1,633
UNITED KINGDOM............	368	454	1,510	879	555	983	2,075	2,551
TOTAL EC-9.............	1,294	1,159	3,001	2,893	1,688	1,916	4,106	4,889
AUSTRIA...................	97	31	14	101	93	36	13	73
GIBRALTAR.................	26	42	51	28	36	98	70	64
GREECE....................	32	0	5	129	24	0	2	65
MALTA-GOZO................	49	469	206	432	69	760	300	587
PORTUGAL..................	1	7	0	0	3	44	2	0
SPAIN.....................	55	107	803	1,044	52	116	1,026	1,190
SWEDEN....................	0	0	0	17	0	0	0	18
SWITZERLAND...............	379	301	541	698	410	339	732	975
OTHER.....................	8	4	3	7	7	3	8	28
TOTAL..................	1,936	2,111	4,621	5,359	2,379	3,312	6,248	7,889
AFRICA:								
CANARY ISLANDS............	2,560	8,843	8,600	7,554	2,742	10,617	10,341	8,997
EGYPT.....................	6	1,302	5,089	4,522	14	1,792	4,495	5,041
GHANA.....................	1	6	15	4	1	9	8	11
LIBERIA...................	23	0	0	34	38	0	0	38
NIGERIA...................	720	1,384	150	817	575	1,845	182	870
TOGO......................	17	34	9	0	11	27	11	0
OTHER.....................	10	115	25	1,532	12	133	44	1,377
TOTAL.................	3,338	11,684	13,888	14,463	3,393	14,423	15,080	16,335
ASIA AND OCEANIA:								
AUSTRALIA.................	0	0	14	1	0	0	12	3
BAHRAIN...................	82	185	160	169	141	277	312	370
CHINA,REPUBLIC OF (TAIWAN)	56	18	126	228	48	23	142	368
FRENCH PACIFIC ISLAND.....	538	1,091	1,402	1,532	659	1,283	1,957	2,137
HONG KONG.................	14,236	16,195	20,767	20,260	11,712	15,385	21,529	21,176
JAPAN.....................	20,287	30,894	39,044	60,321	22,343	40,067	47,622	74,135
KUWAIT....................	459	1,130	1,894	3,197	577	1,485	2,916	4,736
MALAYSIA..................	130	134	302	228	135	148	331	272
PHILIPPINES...............	5	0	35	0	14	0	38	0
QATAR.....................	13	6	20	41	19	10	27	65
SAUDI ARABIA..............	470	562	1,074	1,475	949	891	1,933	2,889
SINGAPORE.................	5,212	9,241	13,808	28,377	4,936	10,069	16,161	23,307
SYRIAN ARAB REPUBLIC......	3	0	0	0	1	0	0	0
TRUST TERRITORY PACIFIC IS	146	515	803	644	172	629	995	813
UNITED ARAB EMIRATES......	153	132	100	195	248	245	216	477
WESTERN SAMOA.............	350	461	978	815	108	141	366	372
OTHER.....................	87	63	125	147	91	103	179	254
TOTAL.................	42,145	60,631	80,659	109,630	42,144	70,797	94,137	131,276
GRAND TOTAL.............	74,924	111,976	141,898	191,682	64,249	118,689	150,470	212,524

NOTE: TOTALS MAY NOT ADD DUE TO ROUNDING.

1/ PRELIMINARY.

SOURCE: U.S. DEPARTMENT OF COMMERCE

MARCH 1982

FOREIGN COMMODITY ANALYSIS, FAS, USDA

TABLE 5.--TURKEYS, WHOLE, OR FROZEN: U.S. EXPORTS BY COUNTRY OF DESTINATION,

AVERAGE 1974-78, ANNUAL 1979-81

COMMODITY AND COUNTRY OF DESTINATION	QUANTITY (IN METRIC TONS)				VALUE (IN THOUSANDS OF DOLLARS)			
	5-YEAR AVG 1974-1978	1979	1980	1981 1/	5-YEAR AVG 1974-1978	1979	1980	1981 1/
TURKEYS,WHOLE,FRESH/FROZEN :								
NORTH AMERICA:								
BAHAMAS..................	273	177	191	135	371	298	320	215
BARBADOS.................	9	1	57	1	11	1	108	3
BELIZE...................	20	23	24	26	28	48	49	38
BERMUDA..................	188	172	120	112	293	292	229	204
CANADA...................	1,482	1,392	1,038	1,431	1,724	1,988	1,398	2,164
DOMINICAN REPUBLIC.......	40	10	42	50	59	14	61	83
GUATEMALA................	3	0	5	0	4	0	0	0
JAMAICA..................	10	11	35	0	11	35	56	0
LEEWARD-WINDWARD IS......	26	39	22	38	36	80	49	74
MEXICO...................	22	50	21	45	28	87	26	62
NETHERLANDS ANTILLES.....	34	39	33	39	54	83	72	59
PANAMA(INC CANAL ZN).....	54	94	242	295	90	196	419	669
TRINIDAD-TOBAGO..........	91	134	273	279	134	250	466	490
OTHER....................	16	13	30	18	24	24	40	31
TOTAL...................	2,267	2,154	2,098	2,468	2,868	3,370	3,293	4,092
SOUTH AMERICA:								
ARGENTINA................	0	167	691	195	0	263	1,130	365
CHILE....................	23	145	18	127	37	214	38	193
ECUADOR..................	0	1	0	11	0	3	0	31
SURINAME.................	4	7	2	0	6	13	4	0
VENEZUELA................	80	184	174	777	115	309	344	1,280
OTHER....................	3	11	54	29	4	21	81	46
TOTAL...................	110	519	938	1,140	162	822	1,598	1,914
EUROPE:								
BELGIUM-LUXEMBOURG.......	59	64	6	12	85	81	12	30
DENMARK..................	1	0	0	0	2	0	0	0
FRANCE...................	28	0	18	0	35	0	21	0
GERMANY, FEDERAL REP. OF..	392	13	13	37	464	13	21	66
ITALY....................	706	100	108	69	897	198	167	130
NETHERLANDS..............	66	61	95	43	93	90	193	131
UNITED KINGDOM...........	424	1,161	811	371	694	1,841	1,660	618
TOTAL EC-9...............	1,676	1,399	1,050	531	2,270	2,223	2,074	975
AUSTRIA..................	64	85	0	83	78	120	0	122
GREECE...................	67	77	36	118	86	114	57	183
MALTA-GOZO...............	18	0	0	39	30	0	0	65
NORWAY...................	2	0	0	0	3	0	0	4
PORTUGAL.................	0	22	53	36	2	122	76	69
SWEDEN...................	4	2	0	0	9	2	0	0
SWITZERLAND..............	156	17	0	149	233	36	0	356
OTHER....................	5	17	0	0	7	26	0	0
TOTAL...................	1,992	1,618	1,140	956	2,712	2,643	2,147	1,770
AFRICA:								
CANARY ISLANDS...........	104	95	92	76	133	140	154	112
EGYPT....................	32	90	746	328	58	145	1,061	434
GHANA....................	1	0	0	1	3	0	0	2
LIBERIA..................	5	5	0	3	7	12	2	4
NIGERIA..................	109	16	33	394	133	14	27	494
REPUBLIC OF SOUTH AFRICA..	0	0	32	0	0	0	29	0
TOGO.....................	22	6	5	65	13	0	10	57
OTHER....................	3	20	14	11	4	35	31	23
TOTAL...................	276	227	922	877	351	346	1,313	1,126
ASIA AND OCEANIA:								
BAHRAIN..................	23	8	3	9	37	16	6	18
FRENCH PACIFIC ISLAND....	28	21	55	20	27	48	98	44
HONG KONG................	309	255	235	129	372	389	251	199
INDIA....................	2	3	0	0	5	2	0	0
IRAN.....................	70	2	0	0	94	4	0	0
ISRAEL...................	0	0	0	1	1	0	0	0
JAPAN....................	308	610	569	746	434	1,132	996	1,456
KUWAIT...................	78	225	123	306	117	308	199	491
LEBANON..................	17	19	17	20	25	27	31	52
MALAYSIA.................	25	20	4	10	32	33	8	18
NEW ZEALAND..............	1	0	0	0	1	0	0	28
PHILIPPINES..............	6	16	0	14	7	29	0	28
SAUDI ARABIA.............	95	150	292	667	196	261	595	1,332
SINGAPORE................	188	213	157	216	226	314	222	349
TRUST TERRITORY PACIFIC IS	13	27	32	14	16	34	42	24
UNITED ARAB EMIRATES.....	40	75	106	146	70	185	227	348
WESTERN SAMOA............	44	2	3	1	27	3	5	2
OTHER....................	22	54	79	147	33	97	129	294
TOTAL...................	1,261	1,700	1,675	2,446	1,718	2,880	2,810	4,660
GRAND TOTAL.............	5,907	6,215	6,773	7,888	7,812	10,080	11,161	13,561

NOTE: TOTALS MAY NOT ADD DUE TO ROUNDING.

1/ PRELIMINARY.

SOURCE: U.S. DEPARTMENT OF COMMERCE

MARCH 1982

FOREIGN COMMODITY ANALYSIS, FAS, USDA

9

TABLE 6.--TURKEY PARTS, FRESH OR FROZEN: U.S. EXPORTS BY COUNTRY OF DESTINATION,

AVERAGE 1974-78, ANNUAL 1979-81

COMMODITY AND COUNTRY OF DESTINATION	QUANTITY (IN METRIC TONS)				VALUE (IN THOUSANDS OF DOLLARS)			
	5-YEAR AVG 1974-1978	1979	1980	1981[1/]	5-YEAR AVG 1974-1978	1979	1980	1981[1/]
TURKEY PARTS,FRESH/FROZEN								
NORTH AMERICA:								
BAHAMAS......................	141	283	224	373	146	327	211	487
BARBADOS.....................	101	262	150	220	98	203	159	351
BERMUDA......................	30	29	6	32	59	61	21	84
CANADA.......................	1,059	566	189	301	1,275	854	278	607
EL SALVADOR..................	15	0	0	0	18	0	0	0
JAMAICA......................	27	0	0	1	30	0	0	3
LEEWARD-WINDWARD IS..........	53	107	177	248	51	98	148	207
MEXICO.......................	207	153	122	178	115	114	101	135
NETHERLANDS ANTILLES.........	16	45	20	9	30	64	34	21
PANAMA(INC CANAL ZN).........	19	9	42	27	45	28	110	63
TRINIDAD-TOBAGO..............	8	103	583	826	13	116	651	875
OTHER........................	6	5	46	44	11	12	70	65
TOTAL....................	1,682	1,562	1,558	2,258	1,891	1,817	1,783	2,817
SOUTH AMERICA:								
SURINAME.....................	0	0	0	0	0	0	0	0
VENEZUELA....................	17	163	74	133	35	280	131	254
OTHER........................	1	154	142	56	1	272	247	82
TOTAL....................	19	317	216	189	36	552	378	336
EUROPE:								
BELGIUM-LUXEMBOURG...........	127	0	0	46	178	0	0	160
DENMARK......................	34	32	19	12	82	67	61	24
FRANCE.......................	5	1	2	0	2	4	42	0
GERMANY, FEDERAL REP. OF..	9,460	8,691	7,091	6,196	12,287	13,472	10,556	8,440
IRELAND......................	0	0	0	14	0	0	0	61
ITALY........................	383	404	71	33	590	768	106	94
NETHERLANDS..................	236	224	282	738	275	330	434	1,139
UNITED KINGDOM...............	1,311	1,831	2,183	1,296	2,989	5,234	6,260	5,495
TOTAL EC-9...............	11,556	11,183	9,649	8,335	16,404	19,675	17,460	15,515
AUSTRIA......................	163	78	63	18	294	151	79	28
GREECE.......................	36	9	27	107	35	38	46	249
MALTA-GOZO...................	2	0	15	4	3	0	30	17
NORWAY.......................	8	5	24	22	15	29	58	142
PORTUGAL.....................	21	17	0	0	63	29	0	0
SWEDEN.......................	47	29	28	34	94	93	102	166
SWITZERLAND..................	665	563	479	116	1,937	858	724	286
OTHER........................	10	3	14	27	12	4	29	102
TOTAL....................	12,505	11,887	10,299	8,661	17,961	20,869	18,528	16,504
AFRICA:								
CANARY ISLANDS...............	99	47	10	0	94	82	17	0
EGYPT........................	5	151	10,570	4,889	9	232	7,981	4,428
GHANA........................	40	0	1	3	36	0	2	3
LIBERIA......................	2	5	50	95	3	6	72	127
NIGERIA......................	1,577	419	2,195	416	1,275	512	2,400	539
REPUBLIC OF SOUTH AFRICA..	2	0	0	0	5	0	0	0
TOGO.........................	369	781	1,184	2,049	322	773	1,566	2,540
OTHER........................	14	138	136	19	12	163	207	28
TOTAL....................	2,109	1,538	14,044	7,471	1,756	1,769	12,245	7,666
ASIA AND OCEANIA:								
FRENCH PACIFIC ISLANDS.....	2	9	3	9	7	25	14	42
HONG KONG....................	723	372	433	691	706	379	618	854
ISRAEL.......................	10	0	5	0	12	0	5	0
JAPAN........................	245	448	284	288	493	920	615	820
KUWAIT.......................	8	44	14	44	13	76	42	138
LEBANON......................	2	0	0	23	4	0	0	50
MALAYSIA.....................	1	2	0	10	3	5	0	16
NEW ZEALAND..................	46	15	4	11	86	68	49	74
SAUDI ARABIA.................	35	89	198	681	89	285	463	1,634
SINGAPORE....................	35	53	36	69	67	104	97	151
TRUST TERRITORY PACIFIC IS	114	111	135	180	80	91	114	173
WESTERN SAMOA................	15	20	15	34	9	14	11	23
OTHER........................	49	3	31	61	69	10	53	165
TOTAL....................	1,285	1,165	1,159	2,101	1,638	1,977	2,082	4,143
GRAND TOTAL..............	17,404	16,470	27,276	20,681	23,282	27,843	35,016	31,363

NOTE: TOTALS MAY NOT ADD DUE TO ROUNDING.

1/ PRELIMINARY.

SOURCE: U.S. DEPARTMENT OF COMMERCE

MARCH 1982

FOREIGN COMMODITY ANALYSIS, FAS, USDA

TABLE 7.--OTHER POULTRY, FRESH OR FROZEN[1]/ U.S. EXPORTS BY COUNTRY OF DESTINATION

AVERAGE 1974-78, ANNUAL 1979-81

COMMODITY AND COUNTRY OF DESTINATION	QUANTITY (IN METRIC TONS)				VALUE (IN THOUSANDS OF DOLLARS)			
	5-YEAR AVG 1974-1978	1979	1980	1981[2]/	5-YEAR AVG 1974-1978	1979	1980	1981[2]/
POULTRY,FR/FZ EXC CHCKN/TRKY								
NORTH AMERICA:								
BAHAMAS.....................	39	54	425	17	65	119	197	29
BARBADOS....................	21	147	151	104	27	271	244	153
BELIZE.....................	3	23	1	7	5	58	2	5
BERMUDA....................	113	80	220	242	185	135	373	400
CANADA.....................	1,562	865	359	374	1,574	1,310	554	845
DOMINICAN REPUBLIC.........	4	4	9	43	9	8	23	67
HAITI......................	4	37	85	0	6	18	38	0
JAMAICA....................	190	766	781	152	89	257	306	98
LEEWARD-WINDWARD IS........	521	356	435	546	618	310	273	435
MEXICO.....................	26	23	86	130	27	34	101	192
NETHERLANDS ANTILLES.......	191	168	110	43	239	214	298	82
PANAMA(INC CANAL ZN).......	15	72	14	12	23	175	45	32
TRINIDAD-TOBAGO............	10	2	446	110	10	4	531	182
OTHER......................	4	3	1	1	10	7	1	2
TOTAL.................	2,707	2,499	3,124	1,780	2,887	2,922	2,985	2,522
SOUTH AMERICA:								
VENEZUELA..................	141	125	611	245	165	213	1,323	395
OTHER......................	5	25	139	203	8	26	233	374
TOTAL.................	145	150	750	448	173	239	1,556	767
EUROPE:								
BELGIUM-LUXEMBOURG.........	6	0	0	246	9	0	0	581
DENMARK....................	0	0	0	19	0	0	0	50
FRANCE.....................	13	4	37	56	23	10	105	104
GERMANY, FEDERAL REP. OF..	28	780	2,393	1,587	45	943	2,981	2,175
IRELAND....................	1	0	0	0	2	0	0	0
ITALY......................	5	0	0	19	12	0	0	47
NETHERLANDS................	16	20	161	786	14	42	378	1,735
UNITED KINGDOM.............	16	267	743	355	42	790	2,461	1,394
TOTAL EC-9............	16	1,071	3,333	3,049	147	1,785	5,926	6,086
AUSTRIA....................	2	0	17	6	8	0	17	0
GREECE.....................	10	10	14	24	20	34	45	61
SWITZERLAND................	20	63	36	52	42	130	68	99
OTHER......................	7	19	0	4	19	54	0	34
TOTAL EUROPE..........	122	1,163	3,400	3,130	236	2,004	6,055	6,279
AFRICA:								
CANARY ISLANDS.............	10	17	0	0	11	32	0	0
EGYPT......................	109	2,246	4,729	986	66	1,238	3,628	748
LIBERIA....................	16	1	4	13	27	6	15	23
NIGERIA....................	137	23	819	487	82	43	705	375
TOGO.......................	246	909	258	429	187	826	260	349
OTHER......................	25	24	5	6	25	27	19	17
TOTAL.................	545	3,220	5,815	1,920	397	2,172	4,626	1,507
ASIA AND OCEANIA:								
FRENCH PACIFIC ISLANDS....	144	117	181	210	242	257	380	461
HONG KONG..................	812	1,016	1,418	702	895	1,458	1,742	943
JAPAN......................	510	753	1,313	724	571	1,477	1,828	1,663
KUWAIT.....................	76	214	76	55	108	359	110	160
MALAYSIA...................	3	20	38	4	6	31	65	12
NEW ZEALAND................	0	0	1	1	1	0	0	0
PHILIPPINES................	1	0	1	1	3	0	3	3
SAUDI ARABIA...............	56	174	351	291	129	364	755	737
SINGAPORE..................	65	174	331	643	91	307	620	1,282
TRUST TERRITORY PACIFIC IS	42	32	14	2	46	51	28	2
OTHER......................	61	183	163	63	100	322	299	165
TOTAL.................	1,771	2,684	3,887	2,695	2,192	4,625	5,829	5,428
GRAND TOTAL...........	5,291	9,815	16,977	9,973	5,886	11,961	21,051	16,506

NOTE: TOTALS MAY NOT ADD DUE TO ROUNDING.

1/ INCLUDES DUCKS, GEESE, GUINEA HENS, AND ROCK CORNISH HENS, BUT EXCLUDES CHICKENS AND TURKEYS. 2/ PRELIMINARY.

SOURCE: U.S. DEPARTMENT OF COMMERCE

FOREIGN COMMODITY ANALYSIS, FAS, USDA

MARCH 1982

TABLE 8.--POULTRY LIVER: U.S. EXPORTS BY COUNTRY OF DESTINATION,
AVERAGE 1974-78, ANNUAL 1979-81

COMMODITY AND COUNTRY OF DESTINATION	QUANTITY (IN METRIC TONS)				VALUE (IN THOUSANDS OF DOLLARS)			
	5-YEAR AVG 1974-1978	1979	1980	1981 1/	5-YEAR AVG 1974-1978	1979	1980	1981 1/
POULTRY LIVER								
NORTH AMERICA:								
BAHAMAS.........	4	0	0	0	4	2	0	0
BARBADOS........	8	8	0	0	5	0	0	3
BERMUDA.........	52	13	112	88	107	16	103	91
HAITI...........	22	0	16	1	16	9	11	9
JAMAICA.........	5	0	0	0	5	0	0	0
LEEWARD-WINDWARD IS....	14	16	44	28	38	9	44	29
MEXICO..........	27	17	14	7	18	9	12	7
NETHERLANDS ANTILLES...	52	20	1	0	36	22	1	1
OTHER...........	50	85	0	0	59	72	8	0
TOTAL........	242	159	190	124	299	140	171	131
SOUTH AMERICA:...........	7	23	48	54	7	65	55	56
EUROPE:								
BELGIUM-LUXEMBOURG......	14	0	65	0	9	0	43	0
DENMARK.........	0	1	6	0	0	5	4	0
FRANCE..........	200	208	127	225	154	151	132	398
GERMANY, FEDERAL REP. OF...	1,443	1,332	1,394	776	1,657	1,754	1,536	984
ITALY...........	1	0	0	0	2	0	0	0
NETHERLANDS.....	34	0	0	40	29	0	0	26
UNITED KINGDOM..	53	0	0	0	44	0	0	0
TOTAL........	1,755	1,542	1,393	1,404	1,591	1,918	1,715	1,438
AUSTRIA.........	47	15	0	0	44	9	0	0
GREECE..........	0	0	0	0	0	0	0	0
SWITZERLAND.....	41	0	0	13	51	0	0	69
OTHER...........	0	0	0	0	0	0	0	0
TOTAL........	1,834	1,556	1,393	1,054	1,996	1,919	1,715	1,477
AFRICA:								
EGYPT...........	48	1,511	612	1,662	33	882	462	1,578
GHANA...........	3	16	0	0	-6	24	0	0
OTHER...........	2	7	0	0	4	5	0	0
TOTAL........	53	1,533	612	1,662	43	911	462	1,578
ASIA AND OCEANIA:								
AUSTRALIA.......	0	0	0	0	0	0	0	0
HONG KONG.......	125	177	107	132	98	173	115	96
ISRAEL..........	32	34	64	11	36	59	47	9
JAPAN...........	25	3	17	11	33	2	24	10
MALAYSIA........	0	0	8	0	0	0	0	0
SAUDI ARABIA....	61	26	75	15	65	48	7	34
SINGAPORE.......	11	16	37	26	8	14	51	21
OTHER...........	21	28	37	85	25	32	42	194
TOTAL........	274	283	307	270	265	329	285	356
GRAND TOTAL.........	2,418	3,556	2,549	3,164	2,610	3,364	2,689	3,598

NOTE: TOTALS MAY NOT ADD DUE TO ROUNDING.

1/ PRELIMINARY.

SOURCE: U.S. DEPARTMENT OF COMMERCE

MARCH 1982

FOREIGN COMMODITY ANALYSIS, FAS, USDA

TABLE 9.--POULTRY SPECIALTIES[1/]: U.S. EXPORTS BY COUNTRY OF DESTINATION,

AVERAGE 1974-78, ANNUAL 1979-81

COMMODITY AND COUNTRY OF DESTINATION	QUANTITY (IN METRIC TONS)				VALUE (IN THOUSANDS OF DOLLARS)			
	5-YEAR AVG 1974-1978	1979	1980	1981[2/]	5-YEAR AVG 1974-1978	1979	1980	1981[2/]
POULTRY SPECIALTIES								
NORTH AMERICA:								
BAHAMAS....................	12	9	26	5	29	35	42	15
BARBADOS..................	54	22	20	15	17	26	34	9
BERMUDA...................	3	18	3	5	36	36	11	12
CANADA....................	1,079	1,634	2,020	2,579	1,587	3,447	4,356	5,649
GUATEMALA.................	4	0	0	0	5	9	7	0
JAMAICA...................	11	1	17	46	20	2	13	33
LEEWARD-WINDWARD IS.......	20	16	7	3	21	22	29	5
MEXICO....................	25	19	22	45	20	21	47	109
NETHERLANDS ANTILLES......	13	5	26	9	29	19	45	28
PANAMA(INC CANAL ZN)......	1	5	0	6	1	12	0	13
TRINIDAD-TOBAGO...........	4	0	26	21	6	0	85	43
OTHER.....................	8	2	52	41	11	4	94	40
TOTAL..................	1,231	1,732	2,219	2,775	1,749	3,634	4,762	5,955
SOUTH AMERICA:								
CHILE.....................	2	30	17	559	2	170	10	395
PERU......................	4	0	0	120	5	0	0	75
VENEZUELA.................	151	7	2	44	159	12	4	86
OTHER.....................	6	1	6	84	10	1	51	199
TOTAL..................	163	38	26	806	177	184	65	754
EUROPE:								
BELGIUM-LUXEMBOURG........	0	0	0	19	2	0	0	165
DENMARK...................	4	0	0	0	8	0	0	0
FRANCE....................	2	1	2	2	9	5	14	10
GERMANY, FEDERAL REP. OF..	12	1,177	1,723	1,790	32	1,940	2,746	3,188
IRELAND...................	0	0	0	0	0	0	0	0
ITALY.....................	1	0	0	0	5	1	2	3
NETHERLANDS...............	61	41	292	1	59	120	938	3
UNITED KINGDOM............	41	61	357	140	61	201	1,431	502
TOTAL EC-9.............	123	1,279	2,375	1,953	176	2,267	5,132	3,868
MALTA-GOZO................	1	0	0	0	0	0	0	1
SWEDEN....................	1	7	16	10	7	98	55	23
SWITZERLAND...............	32	30	65	203	34	29	238	727
OTHER.....................	4	84	104	138	20	338	384	465
TOTAL..................	162	1,400	2,559	2,304	237	2,732	5,810	5,084
AFRICA:								
EGYPT.....................	1	0	149	9	4	0	138	19
LIBERIA...................	3	1	0	0	7	0	0	0
REPUBLIC OF SOUTH AFRICA..	0	0	0	583	6	0	0	492
OTHER.....................	2	0	3	2	2	1	8	4
TOTAL..................	6	1	152	595	6	6	146	519
ASIA AND OCEANIA:								
BAHRAIN...................	0	7	1	37	1	12	6	66
FRENCH PACIFIC ISLANDS....	2	10	16	32	5	26	36	86
HONG KONG.................	38	137	16	392	48	163	65	552
JAPAN.....................	22	12	70	121	42	35	289	344
LEBANON...................	0	16	0	0	0	30	0	0
PHILIPPINES...............	2	0	2	2	4	0	18	1
SAUDI ARABIA..............	11	24	34	142	35	66	87	312
SINGAPORE.................	9	36	15	90	15	50	36	257
OTHER.....................	13	22	43	52	27	32	105	105
TOTAL..................	98	257	197	868	178	413	642	1,724
GRAND TOTAL..............	1,660	3,427	5,152	7,349	2,348	6,971	11,425	14,035

NOTE: TOTALS MAY NOT ADD DUE TO ROUNDING.

1/ INCLUDES RENDERED POULTRY FAT AND, SINCE 1978, BIRDS EXCEPT CANNED. 2/ PRELIMINARY.

SOURCE: U.S. DEPARTMENT OF COMMERCE

MARCH 198

FOREIGN COMMODITY ANALYSIS, FAS, USDA

TABLE 10.--CANNED POULTRY: U.S. EXPORTS BY COUNTRY OF DESTINATION,

AVERAGE 1974-78, ANNUAL 1979-81

COMMODITY AND COUNTRY OF DESTINATION	QUANTITY (IN METRIC TONS)				VALUE (IN THOUSANDS OF DOLLARS)			
	5-YEAR AVG 1974-1978	1979	1980	1981 1/	5-YEAR AVG 1974-1978	1979	1980	1981 1/
CANNED POULTRY								
NORTH AMERICA:								
BAHAMAS........................	7	0	0	0	15	0	0	0
BARBADOS.......................	9	53	9	3	13	35	24	11
BERMUDA........................	13	2	1	1	26	5	3	3
CANADA.........................	629	97	274	244	656	120	391	430
JAMAICA........................	22	0	16	2	22	1	12	29
HAITI..........................	0	0	51	119	0	1	74	126
LEEWARD-WINDWARD IS........	197	0	0	1	153	0	0	2
MEXICO.........................	34	19	21	33	34	12	27	40
NETHERLANDS ANTILLES......	36	1	1	13	34	2	1	13
PANAMA(INC CANAL ZN)......	5	25	20	1	11	65	45	2
TRINIDAD-TOBAGO............	6	0	0	16	6	0	0	46
OTHER..........................	12	20	2	16	20	42	4	39
TOTAL.....................	973	218	399	456	994	274	594	759
SOUTH AMERICA:								
CHILE..........................	6	320	1,429	338	6	441	1,466	364
COLOMBIA.......................	0	16	48	59	1	14	137	139
VENEZUELA......................	4	0	24	32	2	0	66	135
OTHER..........................	7	1	3	16	17	6	19	49
TOTAL.....................	18	338	1,504	445	25	461	1,688	687
EUROPE:								
BELGIUM-LUXEMBOURG..........	6	7	4	18	35	35	19	147
DENMARK........................	3	0	0	0	4	0	0	0
FRANCE.........................	5	0	0	0	9	0	0	0
GERMANY, FEDERAL REP. OF..	78	8	9	38	128	14	18	180
ITALY..........................	2	0	0	0	4	5	0	0
NETHERLANDS....................	28	54	81	27	87	305	288	154
UNITED KINGDOM.................	45	145	97	93	268	614	506	640
TOTAL EC-9................	168	215	191	177	537	972	832	1,122
AUSTRIA........................	2	4	4	13	17	33	30	89
GREECE.........................	9	8	44	55	28	34	94	165
SPAIN..........................	21	0	0	0	131	0	0	0
SWEDEN.........................	3	2	1	1	11	21	7	15
SWITZERLAND....................	30	17	25	7	182	125	196	50
OTHER..........................	5	0	0	0	20	1	1	0
TOTAL.....................	238	245	264	253	925	1,186	1,160	1,442
AFRICA:								
CANARY ISLANDS.............	1	0	15	0	1	0	13	0
EGYPT..........................	15	92	116	0	16	120	205	0
GUINEA.........................	0	2	1	2	0	7	5	8
LIBYA..........................	1	0	0	0	1	0	0	0
SOUTH AFRICA, REPUBLIC OF.	2	1	2	83	13	5	17	152
OTHER..........................	83	0	1	4	76	0	4	6
TOTAL.....................	103	94	136	89	108	132	245	166
ASIA AND OCEANIA:								
AUSTRALIA......................	13	0	0	0	13	0	0	0
FRENCH PACIFIC ISLANDS....	25	29	18	22	23	31	20	27
HONG KONG......................	16	28	9	22	27	53	18	37
JAPAN..........................	58	12	6	7	75	27	14	14
KOREA, REPUBLIC OF..........	1	0	0	0	1	0	0	0
SAUDI ARABIA...................	32	2	4	43	41	8	6	56
SINGAPORE......................	4	2	0	2	5	3	0	9
TRUST TERRITORY PACIFIC IS	109	713	293	84	124	1,891	558	167
WESTERN SAMOA..................	42	46	36	9	28	38	34	9
OTHER..........................	86	29	36	20	88	38	43	25
TOTAL.....................	385	862	402	209	426	2,089	693	344
GRAND TOTAL.................	1,717	1,756	2,705	1,452	2,480	4,141	4,380	3,398

NOTE: TOTALS MAY NOT ADD DUE TO ROUNDING.

1/ PRELIMINARY.

SOURCE: U.S. DEPARTMENT OF COMMERCE

FOREIGN COMMODITY ANALYSIS, FAS, USDA

COMMODITY AND COUNTRY OF DESTINATION	QUANTITY (IN THOUSANDS OF DOZENS)				VALUE (IN THOUSANDS OF DOLLARS)			
	5-YEAR AVG 1974-1978	1979	1980	1981 [1]	5-YEAR AVG 1974-1978	1979	1980	1981 [1]
SHELL EGGS, FOR HATCHING								
NORTH AMERICA:								
BARBADOS...............	258	463	398	409	309	613	572	687
BELIZE.................	41	46	79	29	46	59	109	56
BERMUDA................	6	17	0	0	5	11	8	0
CANADA.................	7,437	8,923	5,854	5,840	10,336	14,353	10,914	9,638
COSTA RICA.............	38	533	446	51	50	715	657	78
DOMINICAN REPUBLIC.....	853	1,655	1,720	534	943	2,624	2,430	847
EL SALVADOR............	57	28	5	2	73	37	18	24
FRENCH WEST INDIES.....	35	20	34	46	38	26	47	73
GUATEMALA..............	3	8	2	5	6	9	28	7
HAITI..................	48	137	248	166	55	186	358	260
HONDURAS...............	75	338	252	27	98	474	373	46
JAMAICA................	2,957	3,032	2,690	2,535	3,023	4,210	3,966	4,062
LEEWARD-WINDWARD IS....	17	7	117	166	22	5	172	273
MEXICO.................	48	881	2,985	7,917	137	1,112	3,355	10,914
NICARAGUA..............	211	322	480	272	243	462	779	446
PANAMA(INC CANAL ZN)...	89	163	69	72	130	316	233	340
TRINIDAD-TOBAGO........	1,609	3,097	2,860	3,108	1,924	4,117	4,172	5,188
OTHER..................	13	23	20	40	15	23	24	44
TOTAL.................	13,393	19,692	18,258	21,219	17,452	29,353	27,294	32,982
SOUTH AMERICA:								
ARGENTINA..............	45	376	2,140	110	630	1,312	3,649	461
BRAZIL.................	15	7	0	11	122	171	0	23
CHILE..................	5	26	58	58	13	79	373	423
COLOMBIA...............	8	29	14	6	39	94	88	23
ECUADOR................	134	126	134	108	154	167	194	267
GUYANA.................	725	996	920	858	893	1,474	1,436	1,469
PERU...................	4	0	0	2	17	0	0	16
SURINAME...............	310	470	524	538	391	682	821	959
VENEZUELA..............	134	1,374	1,560	3,363	186	2,030	2,274	4,980
OTHER..................	1	0	27	46	7	2	124	236
TOTAL.................	1,382	3,403	5,376	5,899	2,451	6,011	8,959	8,850
EUROPE:								
BELGIUM-LUXEMBOURG.....	35	30	134	126	103	86	214	197
FRANCE.................	32	8	34	52	135	27	112	222
GERMANY, FEDERAL REP. OF..	138	167	241	156	436	763	890	871
ITALY..................	286	224	205	315	1,125	1,642	1,295	2,067
NETHERLANDS............	25	70	351	8	101	320	454	1
UNITED KINGDOM.........	0	0	1	8	1	0	2	11
TOTAL EC-9...........	516	500	967	658	1,900	2,837	2,967	3,389
SPAIN..................	7	2	13	13	28	21	59	41
OTHER..................	2	98	798	190	12	269	904	309
TOTAL.................	524	600	1,778	861	1,941	3,127	3,930	3,733
AFRICA, ASIA, AND OCEANIA:								
IRAN...................	5	9	0	0	8	35	0	0
JAPAN..................	28	116	9	5	53	82	13	6
JORDAN.................	0	77	498	0	0	98	1,240	0
OTHER..................	33	104	226	63	99	390	572	305
TOTAL.................	66	306	733	68	161	605	1,825	311
GRAND TOTAL............	15,366	24,001	26,145	27,247	22,004	39,095	42,008	45,872

NOTE: TOTALS MAY NOT ADD DUE TO ROUNDING.

1/ PRELIMINARY.

SOURCE: U.S. DEPARTMENT OF COMMERCE

MARCH 1982

FOREIGN COMMODITY ANALYSIS, FAS, USDA

TABLE 12.--SHELL EGGS, FOR CONSUMPTION: U.S. EXPORTS BY COUNTRY OF DESTINATION,

AVERAGE 1974-78, ANNUAL 1979-81

COMMODITY AND COUNTRY OF DESTINATION	QUANTITY (IN THOUSANDS OF DOZENS)				VALUE (IN THOUSANDS OF DOLLARS)			
	5-YEAR AVG 1974-1978	1979	1980	1981[1]/	5-YEAR AVG 1974-1978	1979	1980	1981[1]/
SHELL EGGS,EXCEPT HATCHING								
NORTH AMERICA:								
BAHAMAS.....................	56	34	77	49	37	25	65	33
BARBADOS...................	0	53	341	36	0	49	293	16
BELIZE.....................	20	0	36	6	12	0	21	7
BERMUDA....................	641	651	630	94	497	412	372	65
CANADA.....................	4,400	4,827	3,744	2,451	2,627	3,163	2,532	1,741
HAITI......................	27	119	106	66	17	90	53	110
HONDURAS...................	0	0	202	5	0	0	127	2
JAMAICA....................	22	11	14	0	15	13	9	0
LEEWARD-WINDWARD IS........	167	314	626	681	110	208	417	519
MEXICO.....................	622	3,230	695	5,343	377	2,058	628	4,534
NETHERLANDS ANTILLES......	154	171	141	472	100	115	106	331
PANAMA(INC CANAL ZN)......	96	0	0	41	55	0	0	37
TRINIDAD-TOBAGO............	4	27	103	3	5	30	152	2
OTHER......................	46	55	515	84	29	43	339	68
TOTAL..................	6,254	9,491	7,236	9,331	3,791	6,207	5,025	7,464
SOUTH AMERICA:								
COLOMBIA...................	3	53	159	355	7	72	162	297
VENEZUELA..................	2,883	22	1,003	1,561	1,794	72	664	966
OTHER......................	6	62	614	80	20	214	690	546
TOTAL..................	2,892	137	1,776	1,996	1,821	358	1,516	1,808
EUROPE:								
FRANCE.....................	7	13	14	39	16	48	68	163
GERMANY, FEDERAL REP. OF..	0	5	0	572	1	10	0	263
ITALY......................	0	14	2	9	0	47	9	0
NETHERLANDS................	16	2	657	4	25	7	479	3
UNITED KINGDOM.............	0	0	0	0	1	0	0	1
TOTAL EC-9.............	24	34	673	615	43	112	556	431
SPAIN......................	30	4	22	2	28	15	25	5
OTHER......................	0	0	0	3,910	0	0	0	2,735
TOTAL..................	54	38	695	4,528	70	127	580	3,171
AFRICA, ASIA, AND OCEANIA:								
EGYPT......................	29	0	966	7,665	30	0	729	5,318
UNITED ARAB EMIRATES......	0	0	6,892	12,150	0	0	4,620	7,653
GUINEA.....................	22	15	35	20	16	12	19	12
HONG KONG..................	6,422	6,965	6,960	10,591	3,791	4,110	4,202	6,875
IRAQ.......................	0	0	12,929	24,568	0	0	8,702	16,604
JAPAN......................	44	90	246	163	47	142	246	266
LEBANON....................	0	0	1,873	4,884	0	0	1,124	3,107
SAUDI ARABIA...............	102	962	9,380	8,001	79	713	5,655	5,732
SYRIA......................	0	0	3,042	23	0	0	1,400	23
TRUST TERRITORY PACIFIC IS	121	270	160	235	72	163	113	169
YEMEN (SANA)..............	201	0	295	0	84	0	147	0
OTHER......................	1,584	58	442	8,652	930	110	601	5,866
TOTAL..................	8,795	8,361	43,240	76,952	5,185	5,249	27,558	51,621
GRAND TOTAL.............	17,995	18,027	52,940	92,807	10,866	11,941	34,680	64,964

NOTE: TOTALS MAY NOT ADD DUE TO ROUNDING.

1/ PRELIMINARY.

SOURCE: U.S. DEPARTMENT OF COMMERCE

MARCH 1982

FOREIGN COMMODITY ANALYSIS, FAS, USDA

16

TABLE 13.--DRIED EGGS: U.S. EXPORTS BY COUNTRY OF DESTINATION,

AVERAGE 1974-78, ANNUAL 1979-81

COMMODITY AND COUNTRY OF DESTINATION	QUANTITY (IN METRIC TONS)				VALUE (IN THOUSANDS OF DOLLARS)			
	5-YEAR AVG 1974-1978	1979	1980	1981 1/	5-YEAR AVG 1974-1978	1979	1980	1981 1/
DRIED EGGS								
NORTH AMERICA:								
BAHAMAS....................	2	0	0	1	3	8	0	1
BERMUDA....................	10	60	79	65	19	153	105	85
CANADA.....................	45	46	29	224	139	154	75	526
JAMAICA....................	2	0	0	0	7	3	0	3
LEEWARD-WINDWARD IS........	6	0	0	2	11	0	0	4
MEXICO.....................	90	49	3	90	278	151	13	405
PANAMA(INC CANAL ZN).......	6	0	0	0	26	0	0	1
OTHER......................	8	33	42	46	35	159	162	164
TOTAL...................	169	191	144	428	519	622	355	1,184
SOUTH AMERICA:								
CHILE......................	4	4	3	2	24	27	15	12
COLOMBIA...................	9	12	26	39	52	50	86	190
VENEZUELA..................	10	33	47	78	50	224	296	342
OTHER......................	3	5	4	8	18	35	30	46
TOTAL...................	26	55	79	128	144	336	422	590
EUROPE:								
BELGIUM-LUXEMBOURG.........	11	8	3	69	50	52	19	350
DENMARK....................	24	72	87	91	112	179	480	419
FRANCE.....................	1	0	2	0	7	0	13	0
GERMANY, FEDERAL REP. OF..	114	436	704	1,810	631	2,971	4,380	5,159
IRELAND....................	1	6	4	4	3	38	29	27
ITALY......................	39	16	134	259	186	116	775	1,111
NETHERLANDS................	58	40	167	82	273	159	621	423
UNITED KINGDOM.............	272	129	355	296	1,226	833	2,028	1,679
TOTAL EC-9..............	520	706	1,456	1,811	2,489	4,168	8,565	9,169
AUSTRIA....................	63	52	71	53	276	347	425	298
GREECE.....................	24	34	30	33	118	237	186	177
PORTUGAL...................	1	0	0	0	5	0	0	0
SPAIN......................	4	12	22	16	17	58	112	85
SWITZERLAND................	181	192	243	184	855	1,050	1,322	933
YUGOSLAVIA.................	1	0	0	0	4	0	0	0
OTHER......................	1	1	1	1	4	7	4	4
TOTAL...................	796	998	1,822	2,098	3,768	6,898	10,594	10,665
AFRICA, ASIA, AND OCEANIA:								
ANGOLA.....................	3	0	4	0	17	0	29	0
IRAN.......................	13	0	0	0	62	0	0	0
ISRAEL.....................	25	31	24	20	127	209	145	117
JAPAN......................	640	1,648	2,638	4,403	2,040	6,717	8,724	12,853
PHILIPPINES................	2	3	11	9	13	25	60	48
OTHER......................	53	208	91	217	166	806	347	1,822
TOTAL...................	736	1,891	2,768	4,649	2,425	7,757	9,306	14,839
GRAND TOTAL..............	1,726	3,134	4,813	7,502	6,857	14,763	20,677	26,478

NOTE: TOTALS MAY NOT ADD DUE TO ROUNDING.

1/ PRELIMINARY.

SOURCE: U.S. DEPARTMENT OF COMMERCE

MARCH 1982

FOREIGN COMMODITY ANALYSIS, FAS, USDA

TABLE 14.--EGGS, FROZEN OR OTHERWISE PRESERVED: U.S. EXPORTS BY COUNTRY OF DESTINATION,
AVERAGE 1974-78, ANNUAL 1979-81

COMMODITY AND COUNTRY OF DESTINATION	QUANTITY (IN METRIC TONS)				VALUE (IN THOUSANDS OF DOLLARS)			
	5-YEAR AVG 1974-1978	1979	1980	1981 1/	5-YEAR AVG 1974-1978	1979	1980	1981 1/
EGGS FROZEN OR PRESERVED								
NORTH AMERICA:								
BAHAMAS	2	3	0	0	.3	5	1	0
BERMUDA	28	37	57	233	34	47	65	279
CANADA	315	766	764	1,285	411	1,035	1,431	2,073
DOMINICAN REPUBLIC	0	0	1,333	1	1	0	1,304	1
JAMAICA	1	0	0	8	1	0	0	4
LEEWARD-WINDWARD IS.	1	0	0	20	1	0	3	45
MEXICO	4	562	549	7,548	0	487	454	9,427
NETHERLANDS ANTILLES	6	2	0	9	8	2	0	128
OTHER	16	17	1,372	66	30	36	394	195
TOTAL	373	1,388	2,744	9,161	497	1,631	3,345	11,648
SOUTH AMERICA:								
VENEZUELA	220	162	107	66	244	249	232	145
OTHER	4	0	3	38	8	0	23	136
TOTAL	224	162	110	104	251	249	255	281
EUROPE:								
DENMARK	3	0	0	0	4	0	0	0
FRANCE	0	5	0	1	0	0	0	2
GERMANY, FEDERAL REP. OF	34	0	69	39	171	25	339	185
ITALY	0	0	0	44	31	0	0	84
NETHERLANDS	14	1	15	322	33	7	52	468
UNITED KINGDOM	30	5	157	118	113	31	763	481
TOTAL EC-9	82	11	241	517	316	63	1,154	1,220
ICELAND	2	0	0	0	2	0	0	0
NORWAY	4	18	0	0	6	53	0	0
SPAIN	0	0	12	0	6	0	26	0
SWEDEN	28	0	0	0	60	0	0	0
OTHER	20	137	124	60	106	849	720	506
TOTAL	135	165	377	607	492	965	1,899	1,726
AFRICA, ASIA AND OCEANIA:								
FR. PACIFIC ISLANDS	94	6	24	87	158	15	37	99
HONG KONG	3,780	3,739	6,991	15,841	4,429	4,970	12,483	23,583
JAPAN	0	0	6	6	0	5	11	21
PHILIPPINES	5	4	2	29	0	0	0	40
TRUST TERRITORY, PACIFIC IS	30	52	166	1,366	42	64	155	1,416
TOTAL	3,913	3,802	7,180	17,329	4,633	5,054	12,679	25,158
GRAND TOTAL	4,645	5,516	10,411	27,282	5,874	7,898	18,189	38,885

NOTE: TOTALS MAY NOT ADD DUE TO ROUNDING.

1/ PRELIMINARY.

SOURCE: U.S. DEPARTMENT OF COMMERCE

MARCH 1982

FOREIGN COMMODITY ANALYSIS, FAS, USDA

18

TABLE 13.--BABY CHICKS: U.S. EXPORTS BY COUNTRY OF DESTINATION,

AVERAGE 1974-78, ANNUAL 1979-81

COMMODITY AND COUNTRY OF DESTINATION	QUANTITY (IN THOUSAND HEAD)				VALUE (IN THOUSANDS OF DOLLARS)			
	5-YEAR AVG 1974-1978	1979	1980	1981 [1/]	5-YEAR AVG 1974-1978	1979	1980	1981 [1/]
BABY CHICKS								
NORTH AMERICA:								
BAHAMAS	3,418	2,519	2,969	4,570	662	634	970	1,296
BARBADOS	13	0	0	0	2	0	0	0
BELIZE	112	200	81	39	27	51	34	29
BERMUDA	21	8	0	8	8	5	0	4
CANADA	7,740	7,249	8,281	10,361	3,136	4,664	5,401	6,556
COSTA RICA	80	100	72	174	60	121	117	191
DOMINICAN REPUBLIC	1,061	2,042	2,602	1,155	545	1,132	1,529	1,447
EL SALVADOR	350	249	328	193	238	428	666	355
FRENCH WEST INDIES	141	1,345	1,930	1,668	29	252	374	273
GUATEMALA	267	416	400	367	268	571	518	575
HAITI	411	608	603	91	83	106	124	111
HONDURAS	887	587	494	254	238	167	299	233
JAMAICA	50	9	2	8	9	10	7	6
LEEWARD-WINDWARD IS	25	106	414	204	8	36	124	61
MEXICO	517	3,114	3,639	7,301	1,467	3,952	4,459	6,652
NETHERLANDS ANTILLES	379	561	564	647	91	168	155	139
NICARAGUA	2,041	353	1,329	2,029	384	79	256	744
PANAMA CANAL ZN	49	42	37	79	57	85	95	133
TRINIDAD-TOBAGO	231	286	307	288	141	205	194	197
OTHER	21	91	42	110	4	55	7	26
TOTAL	17,814	19,885	24,215	29,538	7,452	12,722	15,329	19,029
SOUTH AMERICA:								
ARGENTINA	3	96	457	219	26	545	1,192	1,159
BOLIVIA	1	45	9	5	16	61	8	6
BRAZIL	271	304	557	834	1,468	2,500	4,508	6,488
CHILE	106	178	123	57	169	297	239	183
COLOMBIA	251	190	230	261	556	600	884	1,076
ECUADOR	276	332	381	466	313	462	682	898
GUYANA	220	414	247	251	97	217	136	154
PERU	130	165	146	91	476	683	822	417
SURINAME	1,392	1,089	1,078	1,000	296	272	317	356
VENEZUELA	824	509	540	923	1,029	1,552	1,771	2,652
OTHER	5	0	0	0	12	0	0	0
TOTAL	3,488	3,325	3,768	3,908	4,477	7,188	10,368	13,172
EUROPE:								
BELGIUM-LUXEMBOURG	79	82	75	43	78	134	124	67
DENMARK	4	11	18	11	11	37	94	45
FRANCE	167	223	300	586	738	1,079	770	1,189
GERMANY, FEDERAL REP. OF	5	22	1	6	13	75	4	25
IRELAND	31	23	0	30	65	26	0	288
ITALY	308	136	257	238	486	282	476	484
NETHERLANDS	125	169	195	267	218	521	675	994
UNITED KINGDOM	60	113	55	66	313	519	236	329
TOTAL EC-9	787	777	896	1,247	1,523	2,674	2,379	3,341
GREECE	128	129	262	252	224	262	590	669
PORTUGAL	50	49	30	24	44	89	86	91
SPAIN	305	329	468	379	1,054	1,794	1,989	2,150
SWEDEN	3	0	0	18	7	0	0	26
OTHER	30	158	161	111	237	1,033	1,094	785
TOTAL	1,282	1,433	1,757	1,831	3,468	5,851	6,133	7,042
AFRICA:								
ANGOLA	1	0	0	0	2	0	0	0
GHANA	4	15	12	9	7	41	41	153
NIGERIA	72	20	50	29	179	27	131	85
TANZANIA	1	0	0	0	1	0	0	0
TUNISIA	13	0	0	0	15	0	0	0
OTHER	52	60	117	113	86	298	367	443
TOTAL	143	95	188	151	292	367	539	681
ASIA AND OCEANIA:								
CHINA, REPUBLIC OF (TAIWAN)	437	332	147	132	559	677	463	580
CYPRUS	7	0	3	17	9	0	6	141
FRENCH PACIFIC ISLANDS	69	19	12	30	27	22	18	25
HONG KONG	9	1	1	13	9	2	2	48
INDIA	14	11	77	56	49	113	154	290
INDONESIA	147	252	603	513	365	673	1,667	1,977
IRAN	296	252	0	0	527	456	0	0
JAPAN	1,712	1,054	628	861	3,119	3,681	3,406	3,989
JORDAN	39	51	121	45	44	66	80	113
KOREA, REPUBLIC OF	85	306	79	135	246	1,802	380	373
LEBANON	82	68	33	30	132	142	128	134
MALAYSIA	151	210	174	77	199	307	259	126
PAKISTAN	79	86	165	239	143	144	362	633
PHILIPPINES	319	232	218	281	586	765	838	1,209
SINGAPORE	201	375	389	204	318	618	665	467
SOUTH VIETNAM	21	0	0	0	22	0	0	0
SRI LANKA (CEYLON)	15	27	22	19	34	69	63	36
THAILAND	371	645	689	595	674	1,585	1,796	1,992
TURKEY	80	99	60	80	185	250	351	549
OTHER	88	180	373	256	247	273	762	714
TOTAL	4,225	4,122	3,794	3,586	7,495	16,845	11,401	13,394
GRAND TOTAL	26,948	28,856	33,714	39,013	23,202	36,974	43,968	53,536

NOTE: TOTALS MAY NOT ADD DUE TO ROUNDING.

1/ PRELIMINARY.

SOURCE: U.S. DEPARTMENT OF COMMERCE

MARCH 1982

FOREIGN COMMODITY ANALYSIS, FAS, USDA

19

TABLE 16.—TURKEY POULTS: U.S. EXPORTS BY COUNTRY OF DESTINATION,
AVERAGE 1974-78, ANNUAL 1979-81

COMMODITY AND COUNTRY OF DESTINATION	QUANTITY (IN THOUSAND HEAD)				VALUE (IN THOUSANDS OF DOLLARS)			
	5-YEAR AVG 1974-1978	1979	1980	1981 1/	5-YEAR AVG 1974-1978	1979	1980	1981 1/
TURKEY POULTS								
NORTH AMERICA:								
CANADA	781	1,426	439	1,122	446	1,066	393	81
EL SALVADOR	4	5	1	20	27	39	9	32
GUATEMALA	2	2	5	28	7	10	9	0
MEXICO	29	47	107	238	25	56	121	202
NETHERLAND ANTILLES	0	0	0	0	0	0	0	0
PANAMA INC CANAL ZN	0	0	0	0	1	3	0	0
OTHER	3	3	32	23	13	23	49	15
TOTAL	810	1,482	583	1,432	518	1,194	580	1,223
SOUTH AMERICA:								
BRAZIL	2	0	0	0	8	0	0	0
CHILE	0	0	0	0	0	0	0	0
COLOMBIA	2	12	18	0	9	9	13	0
ECUADOR	3	1	3	17	6	35	16	38
PERU	12	20	20	30	32	4	29	21
VENEZUELA	14	1	0	31	29	27	2	42
OTHER	1	4	0	0	5	27	2	0
TOTAL	33	39	41	78	94	83	59	100
EUROPE:								
ITALY	0	0	0	42	0	0	0	56
UNITED KINGDOM	2	0	7	8	7	0	105	0
TOTAL EC-9	2	0	7	42	8	0	105	56
GREECE	1	0	0	0	3	0	0	0
SPAIN	2	0	0	0	1	0	0	0
OTHER	0	14	0	7	0	29	0	36
TOTAL	5	14	7	49	15	29	105	92
AFRICA:								
TOTAL	0	0	0	0	0	0	0	0
ASIA AND OCEANIA:								
JAPAN	14	1	0	10	17	2	0	4
KOREA, REPUBLIC OF	0	0	0	3	0	0	0	5
PHILIPPINES	2	0	0	2	0	0	0	0
OTHER	16	32	3	0	25	13	5	3
TOTAL	32	33	3	15	44	14	5	12
GRAND TOTAL	879	1,568	635	1,545	668	1,328	749	1,437

NOTE: TOTALS MAY NOT ADD DUE TO ROUNDING.

1/ PRELIMINARY.

SOURCE: U.S. DEPARTMENT OF COMMERCE

MARCH 1982

FOREIGN COMMODITY ANALYSIS, FAS, USDA

TABLE 17.--OTHER LIVE POULTRY: U.S. EXPORTS BY COUNTRY OF DESTINATION

AVERAGE 1974-78, ANNUAL 1979-81

COMMODITY AND COUNTRY OF DESTINATION	QUANTITY (IN THOUSAND HEAD)				VALUE (IN THOUSANDS OF DOLLARS)			
	5-YEAR AVG 1974-1978 1/	1979	1980	1981 2/	5-YEAR AVG 1974-1978	1979	1980	1981 2/
OTHER LIVE POULTRY								
NORTH AMERICA:								
BAHAMAS..................	38	84	141	36	96	458	286	95
CANADA..................	11,949	5,784	3,007	4,395	4,356	2,509	2,170	3,720
EL SALVADOR.............	1	4	3	0	4	3	2	5
FRENCH WEST INDIES......	124	22	6	19	119	88	28	36
HAITI...................	21	6	0	15	27	13	3	40
HONDURAS................	1	0	0	3	4	1	1	4
JAMAICA.................	8	7	10	16	16	6	9	34
LEEWARD-WINDWARD IS.....	54	0	23	1	29	0	37	1
MEXICO..................	167	213	612	770	156	334	1,030	654
NETHERLANDS ANTILLES....	145	18	0	43	112	49	0	36
NICARAGUA...............	2	0	0	0	2	0	0	0
TRINIDAD-TOBAGO.........	2	4	4	7	11	16	5	10
OTHER...................	27	19	18	7	40	36	49	13
TOTAL..............	12,539	6,164	3,824	7,314	4,971	3,508	3,622	4,656
SOUTH AMERICA:								
CHILE...................	0	0	0	0	1	0	1	0
COLOMBIA................	1	9	17	3	7	8	32	7
PERU....................	0	0	1	0	0	0	1	0
SURINAME................	20	4	7	8	48	6	10	11
VENEZUELA...............	319	36	35	12	206	45	45	24
OTHER...................	5	6	5	2	24	5	5	2
TOTAL..............	345	55	65	24	286	64	94	43
EUROPE:								
FRANCE..................	0	0	0	18	3	2	0	13
GERMANY, FEDERAL REP. OF..	0	0	0	0	0	0	10	0
ITALY...................	0	1	8	0	0	3	8	0
NETHERLANDS.............	1	1	0	5	1	1	0	7
UNITED KINGDOM..........	1	0	5	1	2	1	7	1
TOTAL EC-9........	2	2	17	24	6	7	25	21
SPAIN...................	4	0	0	0	1	0	0	0
OTHER...................	0	0	0	0	0	1	0	0
TOTAL..............	7	2	17	24	7	7	25	21
AFRICA, ASIA, AND OCEANIA:								
CHINA, REPUBLIC OF (TAIWAN	5	5	0	21	4	10	0	29
FRENCH PACIFIC ISLANDS....	2	8	2	5	1	0	2	12
HONG KONG...............	38	0	0	0	12	0	0	7
JAPAN...................	362	34	10	10	178	42	23	17
KOREA, REPUBLIC OF......	0	0	0	1	0	0	0	3
PHILIPPINES.............	4	9	0	0	20	48	3	0
THAILAND................	0	0	0	0	0	0	0	2
OTHER...................	11	20	3	1	16	40	3	2
TOTAL..............	421	66	15	44	232	140	31	67
GRAND TOTAL...........	13,315	6,288	3,919	7,406	5,496	3,720	3,773	4,780

NOTE: TOTALS MAY NOT ADD DUE TO ROUNDING.

1/ REPORTED IN POUNDS PRIOR TO 1978. 2/ PRELIMINARY.

SOURCE: U.S. DEPARTMENT OF COMMERCE *

TABLE 18.--POULTRY PRODUCTS: U.S. IMPORTS, QUANTITY AND VALUE,

AVERAGE 1974-78, ANNUAL 1979-81

COMMODITY	QUANTITY (IN METRIC TONS UNLESS OTHERWISE SHOWN)				VALUE (IN THOUSANDS OF DOLLARS)			
	5-YEAR AVG 1974-1978	1979	1980	1981 1/	5-YEAR AVG 1974-1978	1979	1980	1981 1/
IMPORTS								
POULTRY MEAT 2/								
CHICKENS, DUCKS, ETC. INCL. GAME								
FRESH OR FROZEN........	85	241	538	426	251	689	1,073	1,408
TURKEYS, FRESH OR FROZEN....	3	1	35	20	8	0	18	11
CHICKENS, DUCKS, ETC. INCL. GAME								
PREPARED OR PRESERVED, NE	195	26	162	134	646	209	491	776
GOOSE LIVER PRODUCTS......	63	39	32	42	957	1,056	1,117	1,172
TOTAL..................	345	307	761	621	1,861	1,955	2,699	3,371
EGGS								
CHICKEN IN SHELL (1000 DOZ)	9,142	9,393	5,052	4,490	2,885	2,489	2,595	2,698
OTHER IN SHELL (1000 DOZ).	729	868	913	954	1,410	1,940	2,424	2,635
DRIED....................	0	5	0	19	1	4	0	22
FROZEN OR OTHERWISE PRSRVD	34	38	54	56	68	119	149	186
TOTAL..................	0	0	0	0	4,364	4,552	5,168	5,541
LIVE POULTRY								
BABY CHICKS (IN THOUSANDS)	2,920	3,456	3,222	2,784	2,325	3,453	2,930	2,611
OTHER....................	1,145	1,203	2,779	644	860	499	1,222	426
TOTAL..................	0	0	0	0	3,185	3,952	4,152	3,037
TOTAL POULTRY AND EGGS..	0	0	0	0	9,411	10,458	12,018	11,949

NOTE: TOTALS MAY NOT ADD DUE TO ROUNDING.

1/ PRELIMINARY. 2/ WHOLE OR PARTS.

SOURCE: U.S. DEPARTMENT OF COMMERCE

MARCH 1982

FOREIGN COMMODITY ANALYSIS, FAS, USDA

TABLE 19.--POULTRY PRODUCTS: U.S. IMPORTS BY COUNTRY OF ORIGIN

AVERAGE 1974-78, ANNUAL 1979-81

COMMODITY AND COUNTRY OF ORIGIN	QUANTITY (IN METRIC TONS)				VALUE (IN THOUSANDS OF DOLLARS)			
	5-YEAR AVG 1974-1978	1979	1980	1981 1/	5-YEAR AVG 1974-1978	1979	1980	1981 1/
POULTRY MEAT, FRESH OR FROZ:2/								
AUSTRALIA......................	3	0	0	0	6	0	0	0
CANADA.........................	76	241	566	446	223	682	1,082	1,409
NEW ZEALAND....................	5	0	0	0	12	0	0	0
OTHER..........................	3	1	1	1	18	7	10	9
TOTAL.........................	87	242	568	447	259	689	1,091	1,418
BIRDS,PREPARED OR PRES, NEC:								
CANADA.........................	189	22	152	98	603	95	323	445
FRANCE.........................	4	4	7	4	39	114	156	195
HONG KONG......................	0	0	0	0	0	0	0	0
OTHER..........................	1	0	2	32	3	1	11	136
TOTAL.........................	195	26	162	134	646	209	491	776
GOOSE LIVER PRODUCTS:								
FRANCE.........................	63	39	29	41	952	1,056	1,076	1,166
OTHER..........................	1	0	3	0	4	0	41	11
TOTAL.........................	63	39	32	42	957	1,056	1,117	1,177
EGGS IN SHELL:								
BELGIUM-LUXEMBOURG............	0	0	0	0	0	0	0	0
DENMARK........................	0	0	0	0	0	0	0	3
FRANCE.........................	4	19	41	132	13	60	152	451
GERMANY, FEDERAL REP. OF..	0	20	2	2	1	35	3	4
IRELAND........................	1	113	0	0	1	82	0	0
ITALY..........................	0	0	0	0	0	0	0	0
NETHERLANDS....................	5	11	10	16	10	23	21	43
UNITED KINGDOM.................	2	1,876	1	1	11	645	2	2
TOTAL EC-9....................	13	2,040	52	151	37	845	178	503
AUSTRALIA......................	0	0	7	36	0	0	0	14
CANADA.........................	5,832	483	5,263	4,685	2,935	1,360	3,760	3,728
CHINA (MAINLAND)...............	227	142	157	144	274	250	279	273
CHINA REPUBLIC OF (TAIWAN)	202	318	324	249	273	463	482	525
HONG KONG......................	67	93	149	137	108	157	276	236
JAPAN..........................	3	0	0	2	4	0	0	1
MEXICO.........................	430	0	0	0	177	0	0	0
NICARAGUA......................	50	0	0	0	16	0	0	0
SWEDEN.........................	1	0	0	0	1	0	0	0
VENEZUELA......................	0	526	0	0	0	282	0	0
OTHER..........................	3,045	6,741	21	40	471	1,073	43	53
TOTAL.........................	9,870	10,262	5,966	5,444	4,295	4,429	5,019	5,333
EGGS DRIED:								
CANADA.........................	0	0	0	18	0	0	0	21
DENMARK........................	0	0	0	0	0	0	0	0
GERMANY, FEDERAL REP. OF..	0	0	0	0	0	0	0	0
OTHER..........................	0	5	0	1	1	4	0	0
TOTAL.........................	0	5	0	19	1	4	0	22
EGGS, FROZEN OR PRESERVED:								
CHINA REPUBLIC OF (TAIWAN)	19	24	26	38	44	64	79	117
DENMARK........................	0	0	0	0	0	0	0	0
JAPAN..........................	4	6	5	7	12	26	23	22
REPUBLIC OF SOUTH AFRICA..	0	0	0	0	0	1	0	0
OTHER..........................	11	8	23	11	12	28	47	46
TOTAL.........................	34	38	54	56	68	119	149	186
POULTRY, LIVE BABY CHICKS:								
CANADA.........................	2,920	3,456	3,222	2,782	2,324	3,447	2,921	2,604
OTHER..........................	0	0	0	2	1	6	8	6
TOTAL.........................	2,920	3,456	3,222	2,784	2,325	3,453	2,938	2,611
OTHER LIVE POULTRY:								
CANADA.........................	1,143	1,283	2,778	642	814	479	1,200	395
OTHER..........................	1	0	1	2	47	20	23	31
TOTAL.........................	1,145	1,283	2,779	644	860	499	1,222	426

NOTE: TOTALS MAY NOT ADD DUE TO ROUNDING.

1/ PRELIMINARY. 2/ INCLUDES CHICKENS, TURKEYS, GUINEAS, DUCKS, AND SMALL GAME.

SOURCE: U.S. DEPARTMENT OF COMMERCE

MARCH 1982

FOREIGN COMMODITY ANALYSIS, FAS, USDA